That's My Dog

# YORKSHIRE TERRIERS

by Marie Pearson

FOCUS READERS

FOCUS READERS

www.focusreaders.com



Focus Readers is distributed by North Star Editions:
sales@northstareditions.com | 888-417-0195

Produced for Focus Readers by Red Line Editorial.

Photographs ©: Birute Vijeikiene/Shutterstock Images, cover; Mikkel Bigandt/Shutterstock Images, 4–5; cynoclub/iStockphoto, 6; Byrdyak/iStockphoto, 8–9; The dogs of the British Islands, being a series of articles on the points of their various breeds, and the treatment of the diseases to which they are subject/John Henry Walsh/University of California Libraries, 10; Tom Myers/Shutterstock Images, 13, 29; ti-ja/iStockphoto, 15; Liliboas/iStockphoto, 16–17, 22–23, 27; grase/iStockphoto, 18; Artush/Shutterstock Images, 20; scorpp/iStockphoto, 24

**ISBN**
978-1-63517-545-5 (hardcover)
978-1-63517-617-9 (paperback)
978-1-63517-761-9 (ebook pdf)
978-1-63517-689-6 (hosted ebook)

**Library of Congress Control Number: 2017948134**

Printed in the United States of America
Mankato, MN
November, 2017

## About the Author

Marie Pearson is a children's book editor and lifelong dog lover. She once worked as a dog groomer, and today she enjoys competing in a variety of dog sports with her Australian shepherd and standard poodle.

# TABLE OF CONTENTS

CHAPTER 1

# BIG DOG IN A SMALL BODY

Yorkshire terriers are small dogs. But they have a big spirit. Many people call them Yorkies. The Yorkie's big attitude makes up for its small size.

**Yorkshire terriers are tiny and energetic dogs.**

A Yorkie jumps over a hurdle in an agility competition.

Yorkies love to play. Some may enjoy playing fetch. Others love dog sports such as **agility**. They leap over jumps and run through tunnels.

Yorkies are not afraid of big dogs. They may even try to boss around their owners. Without training, they can get into trouble. If they don't learn good behaviors, they might chew on things they shouldn't. But for the right owner, Yorkies are fun dogs to live with.

**FUN FACT**

**In 2015, a bear attacked a man in California. The man's Yorkie, Benji, bravely bit the bear until the man could get away.**

CHAPTER 2

# HISTORY OF THE YORKIE

Yorkies came from Scotland. People **crossed** many kinds of terriers to make the **breed**. By the mid-1800s, Yorkies had arrived in England. Factory workers in the city of Yorkshire kept these dogs.

**Terriers were often used to hunt small animals.**

A Yorkie named Huddersfield Ben (left) was the father of the breed.

The dogs were ratters. They killed rats that came into the workplaces.

In 1861, the first Yorkies appeared at **dog shows**. They

were called broken-haired Scotch terriers. Their name changed to Yorkshire terriers in 1870. This was because Yorkshire was where the breed's look developed. At that time, Yorkies were larger. Some weighed up to 15 pounds (6.8 kg).

The American Kennel Club (AKC) first accepted Yorkies as a breed in 1885. The AKC keeps official lists of **purebred** dogs. It also hosts dog shows. Over time, the Yorkie breed began gaining popularity as a pet.

In 2016, it was the ninth most popular breed in the United States.

Today, most people do not use Yorkies as ratters. But sometimes Yorkies will still hunt. They will also chase small animals when they see them.

**FUN FACT**

**Dog shows became popular in the late 1800s. That's when people began keeping Yorkies as pets instead of working dogs.**

Many people like to keep Yorkies as pets.

THAT'S AMAZING!

# SMOKY THE WAR YORKIE

Bill Wynne was an American soldier during World War II (1939–1945). While he was in Southeast Asia, he adopted a tiny Yorkie. He named her Smoky. Then Wynne became very sick. Smoky stayed with him in the hospital. She comforted him and other patients.

When Wynne recovered, he and Smoky went to other hospitals. Smoky entertained patients by doing tricks. She even walked on a tight rope. Smoky often sat in patients' laps. She made everyone happier.

Therapy dogs give people comfort in times of struggle.

Smoky's work in hospitals led to the idea of therapy dogs. These dogs comfort people around the world.

CHAPTER 3

# BEAUTY AND ATTITUDE

Yorkies are tiny. They are in the AKC's Toy Group. The breeds in this group are small. Yorkies weigh less than 7 pounds (3.2 kg).

A Yorkshire terrier's coat can grow to be long and silky.

**Yorkie puppies have short hair.**

Yorkies with long hair need frequent brushing.

The coat can be many colors. It can be a mixture of blue, black, tan, and gold. Yorkies with blue coats look dark gray. Some have a small white spot on their chests.

Yorkies have dark eyes and black noses. The tips of their pricked-up ears are usually shaved. In the United States, their tails are usually **docked**. This helps keep their hind ends clean.

**FUN FACT**

**Some countries do not allow tail docking. Yorkies in these countries have long tails.**

**Playing fetch is a good way for a Yorkie to get exercise.**

Yorkies are energetic dogs. They need daily exercise. But they do not need much space. This is because of their small size. Yorkies also enjoy cuddling with their owners. They can make great lap warmers while reading a book.

Yorkies like to bark and dig. They can be very protective of their owners and their homes. When people or other animals approach a Yorkie, it may bark.

**FUN FACT**

**A female Yorkie usually has one to four puppies in a litter.**

CHAPTER 4

# CARING FOR YORKIES

Taking care of Yorkies can be a lot of work. But it is an important part of keeping them happy. Because they are small, Yorkies can be carried. But they are easily injured. People must handle them gently.

**A Yorkie's teeth need frequent brushing to keep them clean.**

**Different owners prefer different haircuts for their Yorkies.**

Yorkies have beautiful coats. But the coats need frequent care. Yorkies should see a **dog groomer** often. How often depends on the length of the coat. A full coat should be bathed at least weekly.

Owners should comb the coat several times a week to keep it from **matting**. Shorter **clips** may need professional grooming every four to eight weeks. Owners should comb at least weekly in between grooms.

Training a Yorkie is important. The dogs should not be spoiled. If owners let Yorkies get their way too often, Yorkies may act naughty.

They may bark a lot. They could snap at other people or their owners. These behaviors can make a Yorkie difficult to live with. Training will make them fun companions. Obedience classes are a great place for them to learn **manners**.

**FUN FACT**

**Training strengthens the bond between a Yorkie and its owner. In return, the Yorkie will share its sense of adventure and affection with its owners.**

Some owners use treats to reward their Yorkies while training.

FOCUS ON

# YORKSHIRE TERRIERS

*Write your answers on a separate piece of paper.*

1. Write a sentence that describes the main ideas in Chapter 3.
2. Would you like to own a Yorkie? Why or why not?
3. In which year did the AKC first accept Yorkies?
   - A. 1861
   - B. 1885
   - C. 2016
4. What might happen if a Yorkie with a short clip does not see a groomer every four to eight weeks?
   - A. The fur will grow long and start to mat.
   - B. The fur will stay the same length.
   - C. The fur will be cleaner.

5. What does **training** mean in this book?

*Without **training**, they can get into trouble. If they don't learn good behaviors, they might chew on things they shouldn't.*

- A. working on athletic skills
- B. teaching to behave
- C. learning skills to do a job

6. What does **ratters** mean in this book?

*The dogs were **ratters**. They killed rats that came into the workplaces.*

- A. people who keep rats as pets
- B. people who tell on other people
- C. dogs that catch rats

*Answer key on page 32.*

# GLOSSARY

**agility**
A sport made up of jumps and other challenges.

**breed**
A group of animals that share the same looks and features.

**clips**
Haircuts.

**crossed**
Bred two types of dogs together to produce a new type.

**docked**
Cut to a shorter length.

**dog groomer**
A person who bathes dogs and gives them haircuts.

**dog shows**
Competitions where different dogs are judged based on the standard for their breed.

**manners**
Good behavior.

**matting**
Thick tangles of fur that cannot be easily brushed out and can cause a dog pain.

**purebred**
An animal born to two parents of the same breed.

# TO LEARN MORE

## BOOKS

Gagne, Tammy. *Chihuahuas, Pomeranians, and Other Toy Dogs.* North Mankato, MN: Capstone Press, 2017.

Karwoski, Gail Langer. *Terriers: Loyal Hunting Companions*. North Mankato, MN: Capstone Press, 2013.

Newman, Aline Alexander, and Gary Weitzman. *How to Speak Dog: A Guide to Decoding Dog Language*. Washington, DC: National Geographic, 2013.

## NOTE TO EDUCATORS

Visit **www.focusreaders.com** to find lesson plans, activities, links, and other resources related to this title.

# INDEX



**Answer Key: 1.** Answers will vary; **2.** Answers will vary; **3.** B; **4.** A; **5.** B; **6.** C